Behind the Scenes

# Robots

CODY CRANE

**Children's Press®**
An Imprint of Scholastic Inc.

**Content Consultant**
Matthew Lammi, PhD
Assistant Professor, College of Education
North Carolina State University
Raleigh, North Carolina

Library of Congress Cataloging-in-Publication Data
Names: Crane, Cody, author.
Title: Robots / by Cody Crane.
Other titles: True book.
Description: New York, NY : Children's Press, an imprint of Scholastic Inc., [2017] | Series: A true
   book | Includes bibliographical references and index.
Identifiers: LCCN 2016050374 | ISBN 9780531235010 (library binding) | ISBN 9780531241448 (pbk.)
Subjects: LCSH: Robots—Juvenile literature. | Robotics—Juvenile literature.
Classification: LCC TJ211.2 .C73 2017 | DDC 629.8/92—dc23
LC record available at https://lccn.loc.gov/2016050374

All rights reserved. Published in 2018 by Children's Press, an imprint of Scholastic Inc.
Printed in China 62

SCHOLASTIC, CHILDREN'S PRESS, A TRUE BOOK™, and associated logos are trademarks and/or
registered trademarks of Scholastic Inc., 557 Broadway, New York, NY 10012.
1 2 3 4 5 6 7 8 9 10 R 27 26 25 24 23 22 21 20 19 18

**Front cover: An artist's imagined
robot chef of the future**

**Back cover: AIBO, a robotic dog**

# Find the Truth!

**Everything** you are about to read is true *except* for one of the sentences on this page.

Which one is **TRUE**?

**T or F**   All robots are built to look like humans.

**T or F**   Today, there are many robots working in factories.

Find the answers in this book.

# Contents

THE **BIG** TRUTH!

## Science Fiction or Fact?

NASA's
Robonaut 5

4

**Ocean One**

**Warning!**
Some of these projects use pointy,
sticky, hot, or otherwise risky objects.
Keep a trusted adult around to
help you out and keep you safe.

**Sony's AIBO
robotic dog**

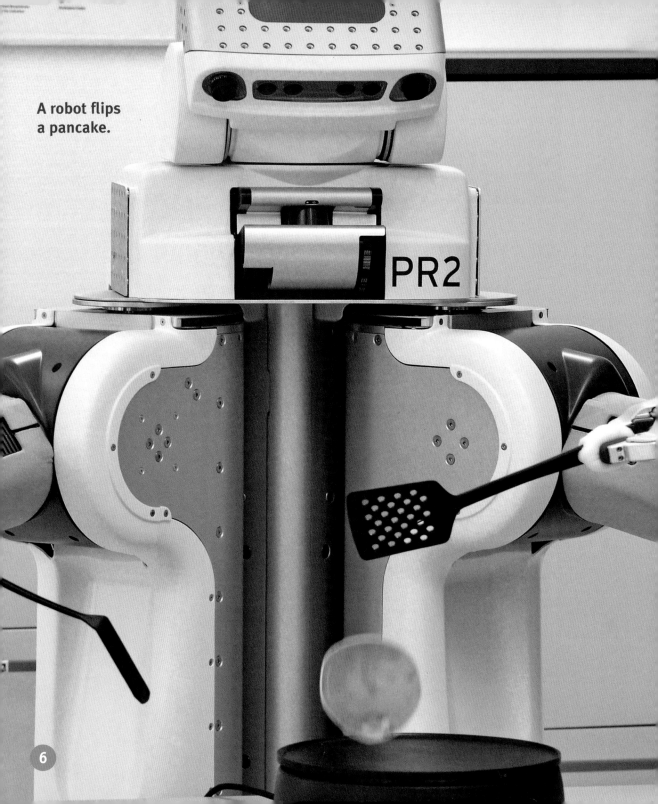

A robot flips
a pancake.

PR2

# CHAPTER 1

# Robots Big and Small

People have long dreamed of creating machines that could come to life. Today, these devices are close to reality. A robot is a machine that can be programmed to perform complicated tasks. Robots work—and sometimes think—all by themselves. When you think of a robot, you might picture a **humanoid** machine. But robots come in all shapes and sizes. And they are quickly becoming a common part of our everyday lives.

The PR2 robot can prepare foods such as pancakes and pizza.

# Made for Fun

Nearly 900 years ago, Turkish inventor Al-Jazari began making mechanical devices called **automatons**. They included a moving peacock and a boat with four musicians that played instruments. These machines were early robots. Al-Jazari's creations were built to amuse royalty, such as kings and queens. People have continued to create entertaining robots to this day. Stores sell robotic dogs, dinosaurs, bugs, and humanoids. These toy robots can move around and interact with their surroundings.

The first available version of Sony's AIBO, a robotic dog, plays with a ball.

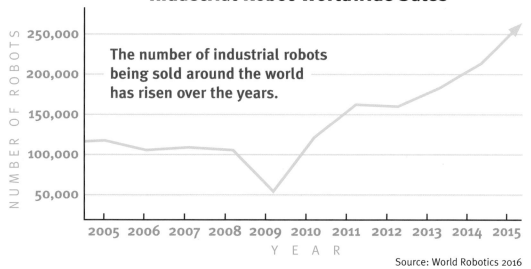

**Industrial Robot Worldwide Sales**

NUMBER OF ROBOTS

The number of industrial robots being sold around the world has risen over the years.

YEAR

Source: World Robotics 2016

# Modern Workers

Robots are not only built to be amusing. Many of them have practical uses. In the 1950s, American inventor George Devol built the first **industrial** robot. It was a robotic arm called Unimate. The car company General Motors used Unimate to assemble automobiles. Before then, human workers had done this job. But it was hard, dangerous work. Robots are now a common sight in many factories.

Robotic vacuums take care of cleaning the floor, leaving humans more time to spend on other activities.

## High-Tech Homes

Many people do not need to look any further than their own homes to find robots at work. Some robots have been created just to help out around the house. There are household robots that vacuum floors, empty kitty litter, mow lawns, and clean pools. Robot vacuums work using built-in **sensors**. These help the machines detect dirt, avoid obstacles, and navigate around rooms.

**SCIENCE**

# POWERING UP ROBOTS

A robot's many parts are wired to electrical **circuits**. Typically, a computer controls all the parts connected to the circuits. The computer is programmed to make the robot carry out certain behaviors. It switches circuits on and off to activate motors, magnets, or pumps. These devices cause a robot's joints, wheels, or other parts to move.

**Diagram of a Circuit**

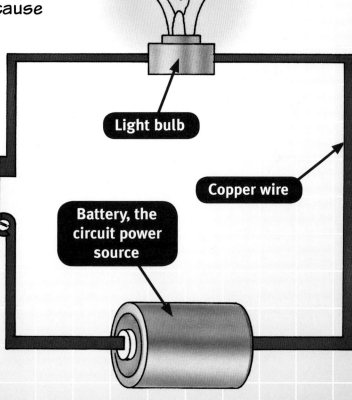

Light bulb

Copper wire

Battery, the circuit power source

Switch, which completes the circuit to turn ON, or breaks the circuit to turn OFF

A robotic teacher, controlled by a human behind the scenes, gives a lesson on robotics.

# CHAPTER 2

# Human Helpers

Today's robots help humans in ways that people in the past likely never dreamed of. Robots can be our friends. They can help us learn. They can keep us safe. They are even improving our health. People continue to find surprising new uses for robots. The latest machines are helping turn ideas once thought impossible into reality.

Saya, a robotic teacher, was developed by a professor at the Tokyo University of Science.

The Da Vinci Xi is a surgical robot that has four "arms" that feature cameras and medical tools.

## Robotic Doc

Doctors sometimes get help from robots when performing complex surgeries. The surgeons use computers to guide robotic arms. The arms hold surgical tools that can make cuts and sew stitches. They can make steadier and more precise movements than humans can. This results in fewer and smaller cuts during surgeries. **Engineers** are even working on robots that can complete operations by themselves.

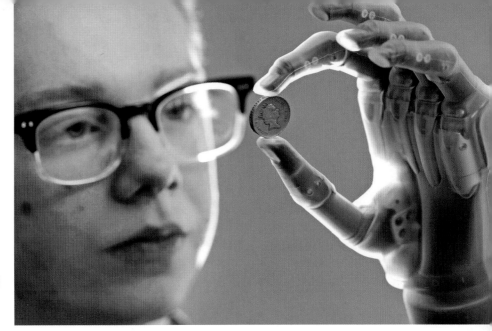

With the help of robotics, prosthetics are more effective and easier to control than ever before.

# Lending a Hand

Thanks to robotic **prosthetics**, people with missing hands now have an easier time completing everyday tasks. A robotic hand attaches to a person's arm. The person operates it by flexing and relaxing his or her arm muscles as if a real hand were attached. Sensors inside the robotic hand pick up electrical signals from the muscles. A computer receives the signals and tells the arm's robotic fingers how to move.

# Friendly Machines

Some scientists see robots as more than just hardworking machines. They are creating robots that can socialize with people. These robots use **artificial intelligence** to sense and react to people's emotions. People could use such robots in their homes as personal assistants. They could be playmates for kids or companions for the elderly. Some restaurants and stores already use robots to serve customers.

A robot delivers food at a restaurant in Suzhou, China.

Being sick may not mean missing school. Robots like this one can allow students to attend classes and talk with teachers and classmates without leaving home.

## Long-Distance Double

Robots can also provide a high-tech way to have a long-distance conversation. These robots stand in for doctors and teachers when these people cannot be present. They are each equipped with a video screen connected to a motorized stand. A person's face appears on the screen so he or she can talk to those around the robot. That person also controls the robot's movements.

robot

A rescue robot enters the ruins of a building in Ya'an City, China, after an earthquake.

# Robots to the Rescue

Robots can even save lives. In 2011, a powerful tsunami struck the coast of Japan. The giant wave wiped out entire towns. Many people were trapped in collapsed buildings. It was too risky for rescue workers to enter these structures. Luckily, search-and-rescue robots were at the ready. These machines are built to roll over rubble. They use cameras and sensors to scope out damage and search for survivors.

# THINKING MACHINES

Scientists hope to make robots more useful by programming them to think, learn, and respond like the human brain. Artificial intelligence could help robots solve problems for humans and work more independently. In 1950, a British mathematician named Alan Turing wrote the first paper to discuss the idea of "thinking machines." Turing even created a test to determine whether a machine could think for itself. To pass the test, a robot needs to trick human judges into thinking that it is human by answering a set of questions. The test is still used today.

**Alan Turing**

A **drone** is a
type of flying
robot.

# CHAPTER 3

# Going Places

Robots are helping people explore the most remote parts of our planet. These machines swim through the ocean, fly through the air, drive on roads, and dive into volcanoes. They help scientists learn more about our world—and beyond. Robots designed to survive the extreme conditions of space have traveled millions of miles from Earth. They have even landed on another planet, paving the way for human explorers.

Octocopters, drones with eight sets of blades, have greater speed and control than drones with fewer blades.

**Ocean One is a robot that has been used to explore sunken ships.**

## Diving In

The ocean covers most of our planet. But people have explored only a tiny bit of it. Some waters are too deep, cold, or fast-moving for people to study on their own. For nearly 60 years, scientists have been getting help from underwater robots. The machines explore everything from shipwrecks to deep-sea volcanoes. They have even dived into the deepest place on Earth—the Mariana Trench.

## Taking the Wheel

In 2011, Google unveiled a car that drives itself. The robotic vehicle navigates, or knows where to go, using a computer. It has video cameras and sensors to help it detect objects in its path, such as people or other cars. Today, nine states permit the use or testing of driverless cars on their roads. Supporters of these vehicles believe they will make driving safer by reducing accidents.

Google's first self-driving vehicle design is a small, two-seat car.

# Safer Science

Volcanoes are among the most powerful forces in nature. These landforms spew fiery lava and release toxic fumes. It is important for scientists to study volcanoes to learn more about when and how they erupt. But it can be a risky job. Scientists have been injured and even killed by sudden eruptions. It is safer to use robots to explore inside the volcanoes and collect samples.

# Timeline of the Rise of Robots

**1954**

George Devol designs the first industrial robot—a robotic arm called Unimate.

**1921**

The word *robot* is invented. It is featured in a play about a factory that builds artificial people called *roboti*.

**1957**

The Soviet Union launches the first robotic craft to orbit Earth.

# Airborne!

Look up in the sky and you might spot a flying robot called a drone. These small, remote-controlled aircraft were first used by the military. They helped observe things happening on the ground. But drones have caught the public's attention as well. People now fly them for fun. Farmers use them to keep an eye on their crops. Directors fit them with cameras to film movies. Scientists use them to track animals and study the ocean.

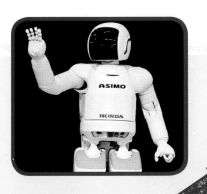

**2009**

**Google begins working on self-driving robotic cars.**

**2000**

**Honda creates ASIMO, a human-shaped robot that can carry out conversations, recognize people, walk, and pick up objects.**

**2012–2015**

**DARPA, the U.S. defense agency, holds a contest to develop robots for search-and-rescue operations.**

# Space Travelers

The United States is the only country to successfully land robots on Mars. Between 1996 and 2012, it has sent four robotic vehicles called rovers to explore the planet. They study the planet's soil and atmosphere. This information will help humans prepare to explore the planet themselves someday.

The *Curiosity* rover roams the surface of Mars.

# COPYING NATURE

Animals have amazing skills. Some fly, jump high, or run fast. Sometimes scientists copy these abilities when building robots. This is called **biomimicry**. There are robots with sticky feet like a lizard's to help them climb walls. There is a flexible robotic arm shaped like an elephant's trunk. There are also robotic penguins, snakes, insects, fish, and salamanders.

## Robotic Kangaroo

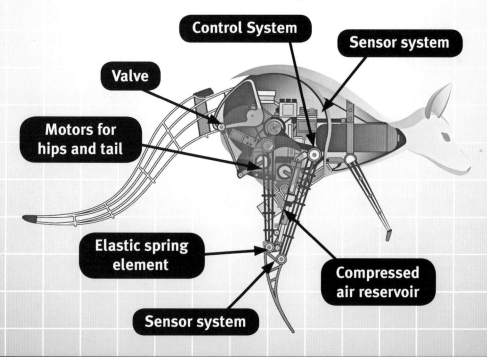

Control System

Sensor system

Valve

Motors for hips and tail

Elastic spring element

Compressed air reservoir

Sensor system

27

# Science Fiction or Fact?

Robots have long had leading roles in science-fiction movies and books. These make-believe robots solve crimes, explore the galaxy, and are considered part of the family. But just like humans, the intelligent robots in these stories sometimes make bad decisions. This raises some big questions about real-life robots. What if a robot does something illegal? What if it hurts someone on accident—or on purpose?

Science-fiction writer Isaac Asimov thought a lot about the ways that robots might change our society. Many of his stories are futuristic tales of robots. In 1942, he created a set of guidelines for robots. He thought these rules would help machines and people live together safely. He called them the Three Laws of Robotics. Inventors still keep them in mind when designing robots today.

# The Three Laws of Robotics

1. A robot may not injure a human being or, through inaction, allow a human being to come to harm.

2. A robot must obey the orders given to it by human beings except where such orders would conflict with the First Law.

3. A robot must protect its own existence as long as such protection does not conflict with the First or Second Law.

BB-8 from the *Star Wars* series

# CHAPTER 4

# Creating Tomorrow's Robots

Robots like the ones in science fiction are still a long way from becoming reality. But engineers are working hard to create more advanced robots. Some are focusing on improving robots' ability to interact with the world around them. Others are finding new ways for robots to move and sense their surroundings. Many competitions are held around the world to let these inventors show off their designs.

 Engineers designed and built NASA's Robonaut 5, also called Valkyrie, in 15 months.

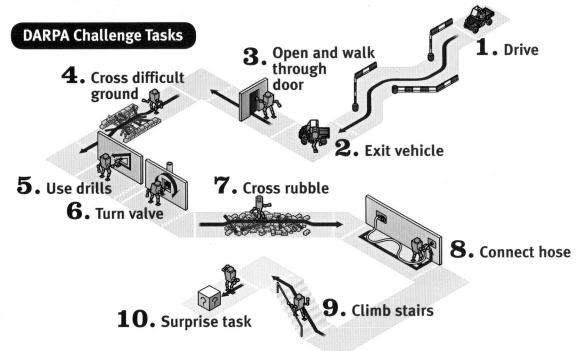

**1.** Drive

**2.** Exit vehicle

**3.** Open and walk through door

**4.** Cross difficult ground

**5.** Use drills

**6.** Turn valve

**7.** Cross rubble

**8.** Connect hose

**9.** Climb stairs

**10.** Surprise task

# Robot Battle

In 2012, the U.S. Defense Advanced Research Projects Agency (DARPA) issued a challenge to engineers. It wanted them to develop robots that could measure and fix damage in disaster zones. The best robots faced off at the 2015 DARPA Robotics Challenge Final. Each robot had to complete a series of tasks. These included cutting through a concrete wall, climbing stairs, and even driving a car. The winner took home a $2 million prize.

# Teen Engineers

Each year, about 75,000 high school students participate in the FIRST Robotics Competition. Teams design and build their own robots. Then they pit their robots against one another in problem-solving challenges. In 2016, teams used their robots to capture an opponent's castle. They hurled foam balls, crossed moats, and stormed tower walls. The goal of the FIRST program is to inspire the next generation of engineers.

David Neiman from New Jersey controls his team's robot during a FIRST competition in 2015.

Robots created by teams in Australia and Germany compete in the 2015 RoboCup.

## More Than a Game

Each year, a competition called the RoboCup hosts a soccer tournament where the players are all robots. The robots pass, kick, and score goals. Teams from around the world compete each year. The contest aims to promote robotics and artificial intelligence research. Its organizers believe that by 2050 robots will be advanced enough to win a soccer match against a human team! ★

# THE LANGUAGE OF MACHINES

The computer that controls a robot acts a lot like its brain. It tells the robot how to respond to different situations. To do this, a computer follows step-by-step instructions written by computer scientists. They may look something like this: $\varpi_j(q)=(q_1, \ldots, q_{j-1}, q_{j+1}, \ldots, q_n)$. These instructions are called **algorithms**. You have likely encountered algorithms. Whenever you follow steps to do a math problem, like adding or subtracting, you are using an algorithm.

# Mechanical Hand

Scientists who design robotic hands want them to move like the real thing. In humans, tough bands of tissue called tendons help people open and close their hands. They connect the muscles to finger bones. Your fingers also need joints to bend. These are the points where bones join together. Try this activity to build your own robotic hand. You will see how its parts work to make realistic motion.

**THINK AHEAD**

How could you use the materials listed to make a robotic hand that moves like a human one?

## What You Need

- [ ] piece of heavy paper
- [ ] pencil
- [ ] scissors
- [ ] string
- [ ] ruler
- [ ] tape
- [ ] five plastic drinking straws
- [ ] notebook paper

# What to Do

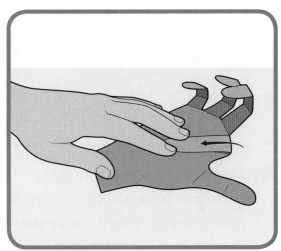

1. Trace one hand on a piece of heavy paper. Cut out the drawing. Examine the joints on your actual fingers. Mark these points on your drawing. Bend the paper at each joint.

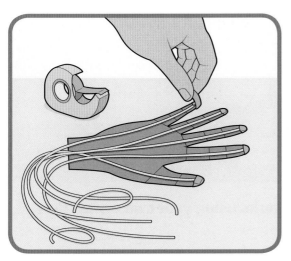

2. Cut five pieces of string roughly 12 inches (30.5 centimeters) long. Tape the end of each to the tip of each cutout finger.

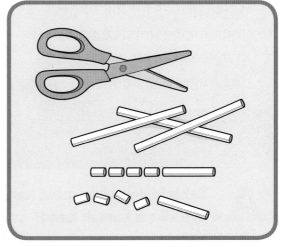

3. Cut five large, 1.6-inch (4 cm) pieces from each straw. Cut the remaining straw pieces into fourteen smaller, 0.4-inch (1 cm) sections.

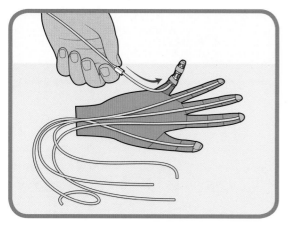

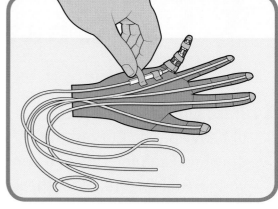

**4.** Thread a smaller straw piece onto the string on your cutout's pinkie finger. Tape it above the finger's first joint. Add two more small pieces for the finger's remaining joints. Leave space between the straw pieces so the finger can bend.

**5.** Thread a 1.6-inch (4 cm) straw piece onto the pinkie string. It should line up with the finger. Tape the straw to the palm of your cutout.

# WHAT HAPPENED?

**A.** Explain how your robot hand works using your own words. How is it like a human hand?

**B.** Was your robotic hand able to pick up the crumpled paper? Do you think it could pick up a heavier or smaller object? Why or why not?

**C.** Think of a task you might like your robot hand to perform. What changes would you need to make for it to be able to do this task?

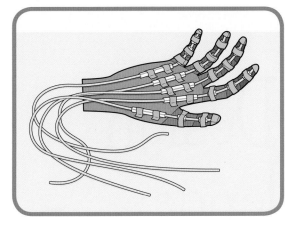

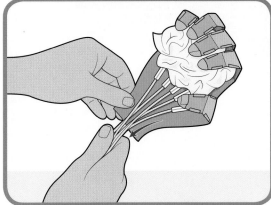

**6.** Repeat steps 4 and 5 for the remaining fingers and thumb on your cutout. (Note: Your thumb requires only three straw pieces.)

**7.** Pull different strings at the base of your cutout to move your robot's fingers. Crumple up a piece of notebook paper into a ball. Place it on a flat surface. Try to use your robot hand to pick up the paper.

# THE TRUE ANSWER

**Each part of your robotic hand mimics a part of a real hand. The folds in each finger work like joints. The straws are like bones. The strings are like tendons. Pulling on the strings is like pulling on muscles and causes the robotic hand's fingers to bend. Your robotic hand can grab a large, lightweight object. But because it is made of paper, it is not strong enough to pick up heavier objects. The hand's fingers also can't move well enough to grasp small objects.**

# BUILD IT!

# Robot Design Challenge

Building a robot requires a lot of teamwork. Engineers work together to brainstorm ideas. They have to design and build a robot's many parts. They solve problems if something goes wrong. What kind of robot would you invent? Try this activity to come up with your own idea for a robot. Assemble a team of your own by choosing a partner or two. Learn what it takes to turn your ideas into a reality.

**THINK AHEAD** — What steps do you think engineers follow when designing robots?

## What You Need

- ☐ notebook paper
- ☐ pencil

# What to Do

**1. Why build it?** All robots have a purpose. The first step to creating one is to figure out what function it will serve. Think of a job you would like a robot to do. Write your answer on a sheet of paper.

**2. Robot needs:** A robot's function determines which features it will have. Where will your robot work? What jobs will it do? How will it do these things? Write down your answers. These details will affect your robot's design.

**3. Brainstorm ideas:** It is time to get creative. Use your imagination to come up with ideas for how your robot will look. Remember, your design has to meet the needs you figured out in Steps 1 and 2.

**4. Design it:** Draw a sketch of your robot. Make sure to label any special parts it needs to do its job.

## WHAT HAPPENED?

**A.** How would your idea for a robot make people's lives easier or better?

**B.** What were some things you had to think about when coming up with your design?

**C.** In Step 5, you thought about ways to test your design. Did this help you think of any issues that might affect how well your robot works? How could you fix these problems?

## 5. Put it to the test:

Once built, researchers need to test their design to see how well it works. If a design has flaws, researchers go back to the drawing board. They improve their design and test it again. List some ways you could test your design.

# THE
# TRUE ANSWER

An engineer's job is to use science, technology, and math to come up with solutions to problems. Engineers follow a process similar to the one you did in this activity. First, they identify a problem they want to solve. In your case, this was finding a robot that could do a specific job. Next, engineers brainstorm solutions. They must keep in mind any limits on their project, such as costs or materials. Then they build a prototype of their design. They test the prototype to find ways of improving it.

# True Statistics

**Average number of industrial robots per every 10,000 human workers at manufacturing companies around the world:** 66

**Estimated number of drones that will be soaring over the United States by 2020:** 7 million

**Total distance driven by Google's self-driving cars as of 2016:** 2 million mi. (3.2 million km)

**Number of household robots such as vacuum cleaners and lawn mowers sold worldwide in 2015:** 3.7 million

**Number of robotic spacecraft in space as of 2016:** 21

## Did you find the truth?

**F** All robots are built to look like humans.

**T** Today, there are many robots working in factories.

# Resources

## Books

Gifford, Clive. *Robots*. New York: Atheneum Books, 2008.

Mara, Wil. *Robotics: From Concept to Consumer*. New York: Children's Press, 2015.

Mercer, Bobby. *The Robot Book: Build & Control 20 Electric Gizmos, Moving Machines, and Hacked Toys*. Chicago: Chicago Review Press, 2014.

Otfinoski, Steven. *Making Robots*. New York: Children's Press, 2017.

**Visit this Scholastic website for more information on robots:**
 www.factsfornow.scholastic.com
Enter the keyword **Robots**

# Important Words

**algorithms** (AL-guh-rih-thumz) sets of rules for solving problems

**artificial intelligence** (ahr-tuh-FISH-uhl in-TEL-uh-juhns) the ability of computers and robots to perform tasks that normally need human intelligence, such as being able to understand speech and make decisions

**automatons** (aw-TAH-muh-tahnz) mechanical devices designed to perform a specific function

**biomimicry** (bye-oh-MIM-ik-ree) the practice of modeling human-made materials and devices on living creatures

**circuits** (SUR-kits) complete paths for electrical currents

**drone** (DROHN) an aircraft without a pilot

**engineers** (en-juh-NEERZ) people who are specially trained to design and build machines or structures

**humanoid** (HYOO-muh-noyd) shaped like a human

**industrial** (in-DUHS-tree-uhl) of or having to do with factories and making things in large quantities

**prosthetics** (prahs-THET-iks) artificial devices that replace missing parts of a body

**prototype** (PROH-toh-type) the first version of an invention that tests an idea to see if it will work

**sensors** (SEN-surz) instruments that can detect and measure changes and transmit the information to a controlling device

# Index

Page numbers in **bold** indicate illustrations.

# About the Author

Cody Crane is an award-winning children's writer. She specializes in nonfiction and has written about everything from hibernating bears to roller coasters. Before becoming an author, she was set on becoming a scientist. Crane worked in different labs, studying heart cells, making synthetic DNA, and testing blood for toxic substances. She later discovered that writing about science could be just as fun as doing science. She lives in Houston, Texas, with her husband and son.